LAUGH YOUR SOCKS OFF!

WORLD'S BEST (AND WORST) SCHOOL JOKES

JESSICA RUSICK

Lerner Publications ◆ Minneapolis

Q **Where does a librarian sleep?**

A Between the covers.

Lerner Publications Company
An imprint of Lerner Publishing Group, Inc.
241 First Avenue North
Minneapolis, MN 55401 USA

For reading levels and more information, look up this title at www.lernerbooks.com.

Main body text set in Billy Infant Regular.
Typeface provided by SparkyType.

Library of Congress Cataloging-in-Publication Data

The Cataloging-in-Publication Data for *World's Best (and Worst) School Jokes* is on file at
   the Library of Congress.
ISBN 978-1-5415-7696-4 (lib. bdg.)
ISBN 978-1-5415-8909-4 (pbk.)
ISBN 978-1-5415-8318-4 (eb pdf)

Manufactured in the United States of America
1 - CG - 12/31/19

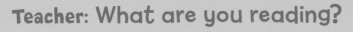

Teacher: What are you reading?

Student: A book on antigravity.

Teacher: How is it?

Student: It's really hard to put down.

Q What has a spine but no bones?

A A book!

Q What is a librarian's favorite vegetable?

A Quiet peas.

Q What's a librarian's favorite food?

A Shhhhh-kebobs.

Q What did the computer do at lunchtime?

A Had a byte to eat!

Q Why do students drink milk at lunchtime?

A Because it's udder-ly delicious.

Q Where do lions eat when they're at school?

A In the giraffe-eteria.

HA! HA! HA!

Q What happens when it gets too sunny in the cafeteria?

A You have to close the cartons!

Shruti: What's purple, squishy, and smells like eggs?

Alan: What?

Shruti: I don't know, but they're serving it in the cafeteria!

KNEE-SLAPPER

Q Why was the clock in the cafeteria slow?

A Because every day it went back four seconds!

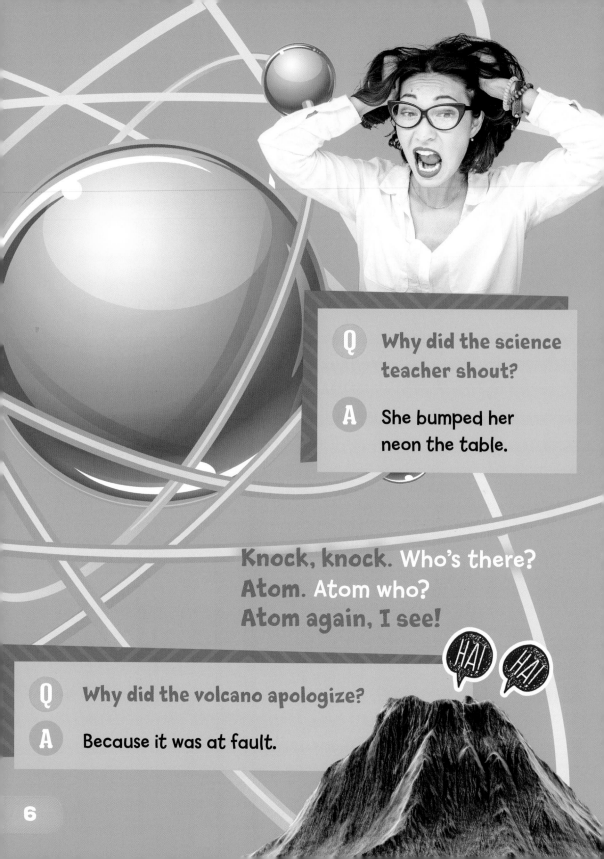

Q Why did the science teacher shout?

A She bumped her neon the table.

Knock, knock. Who's there?
Atom. Atom who?
Atom again, I see!

HA! HA!

Q Why did the volcano apologize?

A Because it was at fault.

Q What did the biology teacher wear on picture day?

A Designer genes.

Q Why are chemistry teachers great at solving problems?

A They have all the solutions.

Q Why was the math book smiling?

A Because someone had solved all its problems.

Q What is a math teacher's favorite dessert?

A Pi!

Q When things don't go your way, what can you always count on?

A Your fingers.

>>>>>>>>>>>>>>>>>>>>>>>>>>

Q How did the math teacher say goodbye to her students?

A I'll calculator!

>>>>>>>>>>>>>>>>>>>>>>>>>>>>

Q Why don't plants like math?

A Because it gives them square roots.

 **KNEE-SLAPPER**

Q Why can't you trust a math student with graph paper?

A Because she might be plotting something.

Paul was about to dive into the school pool.

Wait, Paul! There's no water in there, his gym teacher shouted.

That's okay, said Paul. I can't swim!

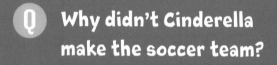

Q **Why didn't Cinderella make the soccer team?**

A She ran away from the ball!

Q **What is a cheerleader's favorite drink?**

A Root beer!

Q Why was the gym floor wet?

A Because the basketball players dribbled all over it!

CAUTION WET FLOOR

Q Why are baseball players so rich?

A Because they play on diamonds.

Student: My sister thinks there are only twenty-five letters in the alphabet. She doesn't know Y.

Q Why was the pirate bad at spelling?

A He spent three months at C.

Knock, knock.
Who's there?
Alphabet.
Alphabet who?
Alphabet you won't let me in the door!

Q What is heavy forward but **NOT** backward?

A Ton.

>>>>>>>>>>>>>

Ella: Dad, look! I got an A in spelling.

Dad: But there isn't an A in "spelling"!

GROANER AWARD

Q How many letters are in the alphabet?

A Eleven (T-H-E-A-L-P-H-A-B-E-T).

13

Q Where was the Declaration of Independence signed?

A At the bottom!

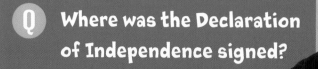

Q Why is Abraham Lincoln the least guilty president?

A Because he's in a cent!

Q Why was school easier in ancient times?

A There was less history to study!

Q Which time period had the most knights?

A The Dark Ages!

Q What kind of music did the Pilgrims like?

A Plymouth rock.

HA! HA!

Q Did you hear the one about the Greek statues?

A It's marble-ous.

Q What is a sea lion's favorite subject in school?

A Art! Art! Art!

Q Did you hear about the art teacher who went to jail?

A He had a brush with the law.

Q What do you call an art student who can't wait for her project to dry?

A Im-paint-ient.

Q Does art class ever end?

A No, it just draws to a close.

Knock, knock. Who's there?
Crayon. Crayon who?
For crayon out loud, do you know where my art supplies are?

GROANER AWARD

Q Why didn't the art student like her drawing?

A She thought it looked sketchy.

17

Q Why did the student bring a ladder to choir?

A So she could reach the high notes.

Q How do you clean out a tuba?

A With a tuba toothpaste.

Q What happened to the music student who forgot his homework?

A He got in treble.

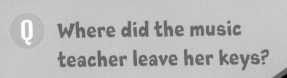

Q Where did the music teacher leave her keys?

A In the piano.

I won't be in music class tomorrow, Mona told her friend. Can you take notes for me?

KNEE-SLAPPER

Q What has forty feet and sings?

A A school choir!

Q How many books can you fit in an empty backpack?

A One. After that, it's not empty anymore.

Q What did the student say after she ripped a page out of her notebook?

A This notebook is tear-able!

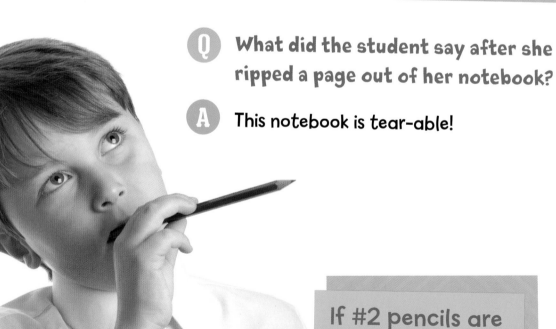

If #2 pencils are so popular, why aren't they #1?

Q What does a robot write with?

A A mechanical pencil.

Q Who is the king of the school?

A The ruler.

Q What do you get when you cross a comic book and a school supply cabinet?

A Super Glue!

Q What is round at each end and high in the middle?

A Ohio!

Knock, knock. Who's there?
Hawaii. Hawaii who?
Hawaii are you at my door?

Q Where can you find an ocean without water?

A On a map!

Q What has a mouth but never talks, and has no feet but always runs?

A A river!

>>>>>>>>>>>>>>>>>>>>>>>>

Student: Mountains make me laugh.

Teacher: Why?

Student: Because they're hill areas!

GROANER AWARD

Teacher: What is the capital of Idaho?

Student: The I!

Q What did Tennessee?

A The same thing Arkansas.